Sacrificial Love

A Devotional

Becky Miles

DEDICATION

To the One and Only, Alpha and Omega, First and Last, Beginning and End - my Lord and Savior, Jesus Christ. I cannot begin to describe the changes You have made in my life. I'm poor, pitiful, wretched and vile - but You love me and You have called me according to Your holy and divine purpose. Mere words are so inadequate to describe my love and gratitude for all You have done, are doing and will do. My Jesus, I love You, I thank You, I praise You - for You alone have made my heart and soul rejoice!

To my fellow brothers and sisters in Christ. Our journeys are all different, but the path we each chose led us to Calvary, where we knelt in humble contrition and our sins were washed away in that Crimson River. Each with a unique testimony of how the Lord brought us out of the miry clay, of how He brought us up out of the dark pit where we once were. I encourage you to continue moving forward in Christ - even when you're hurt, broken and you don't understand - keep moving forward and don't quit believing.

To my FWC family. Knowing who I was when I came to Christ; knowing my faults, flaws and inadequacies now - I marvel at how the Lord has blessed me. Yet, I know it's not because of anything I have done. The Lord blesses us because we are His; He blesses us just because He loves us and He loves to give good gifts to His children. You, my dear church family, are among the blessings the Lord has so graciously given me. Each unique and different, from all parts of the country and the world - but made family by the blood of Jesus Christ. March on in Jesus, continue fighting the good fight of faith and keep sharing the liberating Message of the Cross! I love you all.

For I determined not to know any thing among you, save Jesus Christ, and Him crucified. ~ 1 Corinthians 2:2

For the law of the Spirit of life in Christ Jesus hath made me free from the law of sin and death. ~ Romans 8:2

ACKNOWLEDGMENTS

Mama, you sacrificed so much for me when I was growing up. Thank you for always loving me and being supportive. I love you!

Daddy, I wouldn't wish you back from Heaven for anything, but I sure wish you could see the woman the Lord has created. He has done and continues to do a great work in me. I love and miss you but we will see you again.

HELP IN TIME OF NEED

Satan's attacks come fast and furious, but God's grace is steadfast and strong.

Life is seldom easy, but especially for the Christian, it's made more difficult by all the attacks leveled at the child of God. Satan wants nothing more than to see a Christian's faith destroyed by his fiery darts. In fact, every single trial we go through - whether physical, emotional or spiritual - is designed by Satan to destroy our faith in Christ. His goal - as with Job so long ago - is for us to curse God and die.

Even in the midst of the most fierce storm - howling winds and boisterous waves are no match for the Lord. Keep holding on to His hand and He will see you safely through the storm.

~*~ Let us therefore come boldly unto the throne of grace, that we may obtain mercy, and find grace to help in time of need.
Hebrews 4:16 ~*~

SAVED BY GRACE

"Nothing in my hands I bring, simply to the Cross I cling"....
~ Augustus M. Toplady, "Rock of Ages"

We cannot earn anything from God. God doesn't operate on the merit or brownie point system. God operates on the basis of faith in Christ and His finished work - and that alone. Christian, stop trying to work your way to Heaven. Put your faith in Christ and move forward in Him. Only faith in Jesus Christ can give the Christian the momentum needed to walk through this world as a stranger and pilgrim. Stop clinging to your works and start clinging to the Cross.

~*~ For by grace are ye saved through faith; and that not of yourselves: it is the gift of God: not of works, lest any man should boast.
Ephesians 2:8-9 ~*~

COMPLETE IN HIM

Even if given a million years, there is no way we could ever possibly repay all the love, grace, mercy, kindness and blessings God has showered upon us. No matter how hard we try, it's an impossible task. Nothing that we could bring, no thing that we could offer would be worthy of a holy, just and righteous God. Yet, through the blood of His precious Son - we are accepted, we are grafted in, we are His own. Still, with nothing to offer that seems of any worth - we stand in awe when all He asks of us is our love, our faith, our heart, our life. We lay all of those gladly before His throne, for in our Sovereign Lord, our life is made complete.

~*~ For in Him dwells all the fulness of the Godhead bodily. And you are complete in Him, which is the Head of all principality and power: in Whom also you are circumcised with the Circumcision made without hands, in putting off the body of the sins of the flesh by the circumcision of Christ.
Colossians 2:9-11 ~*~

THE WORD BECAME FLESH

Jesus wrapped Himself in flesh, teaching us that the promises of God will come to pass.

No matter what you're facing right now - no matter how dark and long the valley may be - God will see you safely through. He's done it before, He will do it again. God promised to always be by your side and God keeps His promises.

Long before Christ was born, His birth was foretold by the prophets. Jesus Christ was the embodiment of that promise. God keeps His promises!

~*~ And the Word was made flesh, and dwelt among us, (and we beheld His Glory, the Glory as of the Only Begotten of the Father), full of Grace and Truth.

John 1:14 ~*~

NOT FORSAKEN

The one who stands for Christ never truly stands alone.

As a Christian, we must prepare ourselves for persecution. While it's never an enjoyable thing to think about, persecution is very real and it still happens in our modern times. We often think of persecution as physical torture - and that is definitely one of the forms of persecution children of God may face. However, the most common form of persecution is when family, friends and even some in the church turn away because of our stand for Christ. We must be prepared to be ostracized, ridiculed and made the laughing stock of our workplace, family , school, etc. Even though we may often find ourselves physically alone, we are never truly alone. God is always with us, He promised He would never leave. Though the world, the church, our closest friends and even our own family members turn away, we can rest in God's promise that He is always there.

~*~ ...as I was with Moses, so I will be with you: I will not fail you, nor forsake you.

Joshua 1:5b

Persecuted, but not forsaken, cast down, but not destroyed
2 Corinthians 4:9 ~*~

SAFETY & SHELTER

Faith stands not in believing God will calm the storm - but in trusting His wisdom even when He chooses to let the storm rage.

Storms are an unavoidable part of life. Sometimes they are just shows of thunder and lightning, other times they are howling tempests that seek to destroy your faith and your soul. Whatever storm you face today; whatever storm you may face tomorrow, call on the Lord. Call on Him as the thunder rolls and the lightning flashes; call on Him in the midst of the raging tempest. Call on His name, trust in Him and He will see you safely through.

~*~ The name of the Lord is a strong tower: the righteous runs into it, and is safe.

Proverbs 18:10 ~*~

SATAN'S FIERY DARTS

God promised the weapons would not prosper, but nowhere are we promised the weapons won't be formed. You may find yourself staring down the business end of one of those weapons, but remember what God promised - it will not prosper, but utterly fail.

When Satan hurls those fiery darts at you, try as he may to destroy and devour you - his weapons are no match for the hedge the Lord has around His children. There will be times the Lord allows darts through the hedge, but that's only to strengthen your faith, not to destroy you.

~*~ No weapon that is formed against you shall prosper....
Isaiah 54:17b ~*~

THE GOOD FIGHT

It's so easy to get caught up in the things of this world. We all have the tendency to gravitate toward the spotlight, because we want some sort of recognition. There are two things we need to consider before taking "center stage"...

Is this what God has called me to do? If the answer is yes, that's awesome! Move forward at His Word, His pace, His timing - not your own. Don't let it go to your head. All too often, those truly called of God get caught up in the "fame" and enjoy being "well known". On the heels of this "fame" comes the constant competition, constant comparison between yourself and other ministers. God didn't call you to be a carbon copy of anyone else. There's only one of you for a reason - and that's because you are uniquely designed by God to fit perfectly into the ministry He called you into.

God never called any of us to a popularity contest; we are called to righteousness through faith in Christ and His finished work. So even if your calling from God puts you "center stage", remember that we are called to fight the good fight of faith, we're not called to compete or compromise with the world. Stay faithful to God; stay true to His calling for your life.

~*~ Fight the good fight of Faith, lay hold on Eternal Life whereunto you are also called, and have professed a good profession before many witnesses.
1 Timothy 6:12 ~*~

Everlasting Love

God doesn't love a future version of you, He loves you. He doesn't love you only when you've reached perfection, He loves you in the middle of your brokenness, in the middle of your mess and He loves you through the lifelong process of sanctification. God's love isn't a faucet that He turns on when we do right and then turns off when we fail. God's love is a mighty, everlasting river of crimson red. Jesus didn't die for perfect people, He died for poor, pitiful, broken messes of humanity like you and me. If perfect people existed, Jesus would not have been crucified - because the Cross would not have been needed. Yet, He chose the Cross - He bled and died so we can be found perfect - not because of anything we have done, but only because of what Christ did. He loves you - right here, right now - He loves you.

~*~ The Lord has appeared of old unto me, saying, Yea, I have loved you with an everlasting love: therefore with lovingkindness have I drawn you.
Jeremiah 31:3 ~*~

JOY AND STRENGTH

Have you ever found yourself in the midst of a fiery trial, but suddenly, out of nowhere, joy bubbles up in your soul? It catches you off guard and, as a human, you are trying to figure out why you feel that joy when you're going through such a hard time. For the child of God, even though you go through difficult times, the Lord will send that joy - His joy - bubbling up just when you need it most. That joy gives you relief from the pressure of the trial you are facing and it gives you the strength to keep going. There will still be difficult days, but the joy of the Lord is your strength.

~*~ ....for the joy of the Lord is your strength.
                              Nehemiah 8:10b ~*~

TRUST GOD'S PLANS

God knows your end from the beginning and He alone knows just how it will end. He promised to give you an expected end. It may not be the end you expected, but it will be the one He planned from the beginning. You have free will - so freely choose to follow His will for your life. Seek His face, trust His will, follow His voice.

~*~ For I know the thoughts that I think toward you, says the Lord, thoughts of peace, and not evil, to give you an expected end.
Jeremiah 29:11 ~*~

Go Forward

We must have a forward momentum in all things - especially pertaining to our relationship with Christ. We cannot allow trials, trouble, hurt, brokenness or even our own failures to cause us to become stagnant or go backward, we must continually march forward.

Just as God told Moses to go forward when faced with the Red Sea in front and pharaoh behind, we, too, must move forward. No matter what it looks like, no matter the host of enemies encamped around us - we must go forward. Regardless of what the doctor says, no matter what man's diagnosis is - we must go forward. When the report isn't good, go forward; when your heart is broken, go forward. When your strength is gone, lean on the Lord and go forward. Go forward in faith, knowing God will part that Red Sea; go forward in faith, knowing God will crush those Jericho walls. Come what may, don't stop and don't turn around - go forward!

~*~ And the Lord said unto Moses, Wherefore do you cry unto Me? Speak unto the children of Israel, that they go forward. But you lift up your rod, and stretch out your hand over the sea, and divide it: and the children of Israel shall go on dry ground through the midst of the sea.
Exodus 14:15-16 ~*~

FEAR

Fear is a very real thing - even in the life of a believer. In this life, we will encounter things that make us cringe in fright. If we were to consider all the possible scenarios of what could happen on any given day, we would never step foot outside of our home. We would be too afraid. This tormenting, paralyzing fear is not of God, but of Satan.

We have a very real enemy, seeking to destroy our faith, our health, our families, our friendships, our very life- and one of his best weapons is fear. If he can keep us quaking in fear, we will be too afraid to approach anyone to witness to them. If he can get us to "sit on" our light, he will - because he wants to hinder us in every way imaginable. Yes, Satan is a very real enemy, but we also have a very real God and His eyes are ever upon His children. There's not one thing the devil can do to you unless he first has God's permission to do so. Even then, he is limited in what he can do. So don't let fear hold you captive - Jesus died to set you free - why should you remain a prisoner to fear? Trust in God - He will not fail you.

~*~ For the eyes of the Lord are over the righteous, and His ears are open unto their prayers....

1 Peter 3:12a ~*~

His Great Mercy

So often, the enemy will try to convince you that you've messed up too many times for God to forgive you. He whispers that God can't forgive repeated failure. Yes, Satan is definitely trying to discourage you from turning to God in repentance when you fail - but his main goal is to defame the character of God. If he can get you to believe his lies, if he can get you to believe that God does forgive, but He just won't forgive you because you've messed up one too many times - then he can convince you - little by little, to place your faith in self and turn away from God.

It doesn't matter how many times you've failed; it doesn't matter how many times you've repeated the same failure. It matters that you repent, shake it off and move forward. It matters that you don't quit. The number of failures cease to be relevant to the child of God who repents and continually gets back up. Don't you dare quit on God - He's never quit on you. There's nothing you have done that He can't forgive.

~*~ The Lord is gracious, and full of compassion; slow to anger, and of great mercy. The Lord is good to all: and His tender mercies are over all His works.
Psalm 145:8-9 ~*~

PLEASING THE LORD

I don't know about you, but I want God to delight in me; I want to be someone He takes pleasure in. It sounds wonderful, right? But how do we do that? Proper faith - faith in who Jesus Christ is and all He accomplished for us on the cross. With this proper faith comes a reverential fear of the Lord. It's not a tormenting, terrorizing, paralyzing fear, but a fear that stems from a deep, abiding love and respect for the Lord.

When we have proper faith, we will then also hope in God's mercy. If we want to be pleasing to the Lord we must exhibit proper faith, have a reverential fear of Him and hope in His mercy.

~*~ The Lord takes pleasure in them who fear Him, in those who hope in His mercy.
Psalm 147:11 ~*~

Jesus is Enough

For all the disappointments, hurts, brokenness and pains of life, Jesus is enough. He's more than enough.

Life comes at us full throttle, and we're often blindsided by the constant boisterous waves. We are in shock, we're broken, hurt and disappointed. Sometimes, we are so taken aback by it all that we find ourselves at a loss as to how to move past all the pain. We shed tears, we grieve - but if we know Jesus Christ, we find His strength deep within when we cannot summon the courage to get out of bed. As painful as it is, we just put our hand in His, and with a small, trembling voice, we pray - "Jesus, fight for me and in me" - and He does.

For every hurt, pain and wrong in this world, there is but one Answer - and His name is Jesus Christ. He is enough; He is more than enough.

~*~ And He said unto me, My grace is sufficient for thee: for My strength is made perfect in weakness.

2 Corinthians 12:9 ~*~

He Finishes What He Starts

"God is gonna finish just what He started, even though the water's got to be parted. Lift up your head, don't be broken hearted. God is gonna finish what He started in you…"

~ God is Gonna Finish Just What He Started
by Morris Chapman

God never starts anything He doesn't intend to finish. If you ever question that, all you need to do is look at Calvary's cross. God the Son - Jesus Christ - did a complete work on the cross and cried, "It is finished" (John 19:30).

The work the Lord is doing in you is not yet finished - but it will be. You're going to have to go through some things - but God is going to bring you through them. You're going to face Red Seas of human impossibility, but God will part those waters. You are going to face mountains, but God will bring you over them. God doesn't quit on you - He's got way too much invested in you to quit. God will finish what He started and He is faithful to continue the work until it's complete.

~*~ Being confident of this very thing, that He which has begun a good work in you will perform it until the day of Jesus Christ.

Philippians 1:6 ~*~

Come As You Are

"Come to the water and stand by My side. Drink from the fountain, you won't be denied…"

~ For Your Tears I Died
by Rev. Janice Brown

On our own merit, there is no way that we can come to God for anything. We are vile and undone. However, when we come to God, we come through the blood of His Son, and being covered by the precious blood of Jesus, all God sees is the perfection of His Son. When Jesus died, he died for everyone. When God says "whosoever", He means it. It doesn't matter who you are or what you've done, all are invited to drink of the water of life freely.

~*~ For with You is the fountain of life: in Your light shall we see light
Psalm 36:9 ~*~

~*~ And the Spirit and the Bride say, Come. And let him who hears say, Come. And let him who is athirst come. And whosoever will, let him take of the Water of Life freely.

Revelation 22:17 ~*~

THE LOVE OF GOD

God loves you - whether you're a saint or a sinner. Jesus didn't die only for those who believed in Him or those He knew would come to believe. He died for the entire world...even for those He knew would never turn to Him. He loves you.

When trials come, it's easy to question God's love. You wonder why He is allowing the trial and test. Rest assured, God never allows His children to go through any trial alone. He's right there with you. He won't leave you, He won't forsake you; He's going to see you through.

~*~ For God so loved the world that He gave His only Begotten Son, that whosoever believes in Him should not perish, but have Everlasting Life.
John 3:16 ~*~

The Hope of Glory

There's no hope within ourselves, that is within our flesh. There is Hope in these earthen vessels, though. When we accepted Christ as our Lord and Savior, He came to dwell in our hearts. For the Christian, though just flesh and bone, and having no hope within, Hope came to live within us the moment we chose to make Jesus our Lord.

Christ dwells in you and me - He is the Hope of Glory! He is the Treasure in these earthen vessels.

~*~ To whom God would make known what is the riches of the glory of this mystery among the Gentiles; which is Christ in you, the Hope of Glory
Colossians 1:27 ~*~

~*~ But we have this treasure in earthen vessels, that the excellency of the power may be of God, and not of us.
2 Corinthians 4:7 ~*~

Rest

When I was a little girl and I was fearful or hurt, I ran to Daddy to "take care of" whatever it was that dared bother his baby girl. It didn't matter how small of a thing it actually was, Daddy took care of it for me.

I'm all grown up now and Daddy has been in Heaven for 28 years. Through the shed blood of Jsus Christ, I have had a relationship with my Heavenly Father for 22 years. Whenever something is troubling me, I run to my Heavenly Father and He takes care of it. With gentle arms, He reaches down, snuggles me closer to His side and whispers to my heart, "You're okay. I've got you". That's all it takes to soothe the storm the enemy had raging in my mind.

That's what God wants. He wants His children to come to Him and bring every care, fear, worry, anxiety and hurt. He wants us to trust Him to take care of it, no matter what "it" is. So, with childlike faith, may we all run to our Heavenly Father, snuggle close to His side and rest in knowing He will take care of it.

~*~ Come unto Me, all ye that labour and are heavy laden, and I will give you rest.

Matthew 11:28 ~*~

New Every Morning

There is hope in the Lord of mercy and grace. Nobody is too far gone, nothing is too hard for Him. We have hope, not because of what we do, but because of in whom we believe. Believing in Jesus Christ brings hope because He is hope, strength, help and a million other things wrapped into One. Christ is alive, therefore hope is alive.

One of the biggest struggles for the believer is getting past striving for perfection in ourselves and expecting perfection from others. We are saved, truly love God and many of us are baptized in the Holy Spirit - but that doesn't make us without flaw or fault; we have not reached sinless perfection. We all will fail the Lord at times. It's not pleasant and we hate what we see, but we have to realize there is no power in self to overcome all those obstacles and failures.

I know beyond a shadow of a doubt that I'm saved. I know I'm baptized in the Holy Spirit, I know God has called me to preach - but I also know that I will fail Him at times. Is it a license to sin all I want? Absolutely not! Is it a reason to run away from God - running as fast as possible in the other direction? No . It's a reason to run as hard and as fast as possible to God in humble repentance and ask Him to forgive me. It's a reason to thank God for His unending love, grace and mercy that's new every morning. I need His grace, I need HIs mercy, I need HIs love every single day - and so do you.

~*~ This I recall to my mind, therefore have I hope. It is of the Lord's mercies that we are not consumed, because His compassions fail not. They are new every morning: great is Your faithfulness
Lamentations 3:21-23 ~*~

~*~ If we confess our sins, He is faithful and just to forgive us our sins, and to cleanse us from all unrighteousness.
1 John 1:9 ~*~

His Perfect Strength

Let His perfect strength manifest in your weakest hour.

There are so many things we go through in this life- a lot of disappointment, heartache and pain. In our humanness, we try to fight these battles in our own strength and find ourselves failing miserably. We are trying to fight battles we were never created or called to fight. All these battles belong to the Lord, we need only to be still and watch Him work mightily on our behalf. The only battle we are called to engage in is the good fight of faith - and even that battle belongs to the Lord. We cannot do that in our own strength, but the Lord can. He will fight it through us and in us if we let Him.

We belong to the Lord, we are priceless jewels to Him. He won't leave us in the valley, He will carry us through it. Those angry, stormy seas? He will part them for His children. Those Jericho walls? He will push them down for us - because we belong to Him. Keep holding on.

~*~ Have not I commanded you? Be strong and of a good courage; be not afraid, neither be thou dismayed: for the Lord your God is with you wheresoever you go.

Joshua 1:9 ~*~

GLORY IN THE CROSS

As a believer, we know that God won't share His glory with another. We also know that in ourselves, we have nothing to boast of - it's only what comes by the way of faith and grace.

It's not about our wisdom, it's about God's wisdom. It's not about our might, it's about God's might. It's not about our earthly riches, it's about the riches of God in Christ Jesus.

~*~ But let him who glories glory in this, that he understandeth and knows Me, that I am the Lord which exercise lovingkindness, judgement and righteousness in the Earth; for in these things I delight, saith the Lord.
Joshua 1:9 ~*~

Looking Unto Jesus

Child of God, know this: there will be times in your Christian walk when you will fail the Lord. Failure is never a pleasant thing, as it can often bring pain, suffering and even cause you to wonder if you are saved. You wonder if God can truly love someone who keeps failing. Satan tells you to curse God and die because there is no hope.

God doesn't count you out when you fail. He is waiting to catch you in His very capable arms and wrap you in His grace and mercy, but there are two conditions.

You have to repent. Unrepented sin is unforgiven sin. Don't let your failure stand between you and God. Many say repentance is an act of brokenness before God and then turning your back on sin. In some regard, they are right. However, it goes deeper than that. Repentance is turning away from sin, but not in the way most think. Repentance is first an act of the heart. It's turning your heart away from sin. It means you want nothing to do with sin and when you do fail the Lord again, you will loathe what you see. Repentance is more than an outward "show", it's an inward change, an inner turning away from sin.

You have to get back up. Satan is so busy trying to trip us up and get us to move our faith from Christ. He also constantly seeks to move our focus from Christ and His finished work. So he goes about trying to keep you focused on your failures. Acknowledge them and repent, but don't focus on them.

We need constant reminders to look to Jesus. We get so worried and worked up over things we cannot control or understand. We need to stop trying to figure it all out and start looking unto Jesus.

We all are going to face trials and tests. Yet, we must remember that God is allowing the tests for a reason. The child of God never goes through anything that God hasn't ordained for a specific purpose. We may not always know what that purpose is, but that doesn't matter. God does not require us to understand, He requires our faith to be in Christ and His finished work.

These tests are also here to strengthen our faith. Jesus is faithful. He is the Author (Originator) of our faith. This means any faith we have isn't our own, but has been given by Christ. He gives every man the measure of faith (Romans 12:3).

Jesus is also the Finisher of our faith. He's the One perfecting not only our faith, but He's perfecting (sanctifying) us through our tests and trials. Trust Him to do the work. After all, He's not an apprentice, but an expert.

~*~ Looking unto Jesus, the Author and Finisher of our faith….
Hebrews 12:2 ~*~

The War on Your Mind

The believer is a target for Satan and Satan's favorite tactic is to wage war on our minds. He will bombard our minds with irrational thoughts and whisper lies in our ears. He catches us at our weakest moments and starts hurling those fiery darts. He throws darts of condemnation and ridicule and never ceases to remind us of our failures. He will tell us that we've messed up too many times, God has run out of mercy and grace for us and there's no way God could ever forgive us for committing the same sin more than once. He does his best to convince us that God doesn't love us when we're "bad", that He only loves us when we are "good" and keep all the commandments perfectly. He accuses us of not being saved and at times even attempts to get us to believe that God is just sitting in Heaven, waiting for us to make one wrong move and He will strike us dead. He attempts to have us live in the past - our past sins, our past mistakes, our past failures, our past hurts. He is the accuser of the brethren and sadly, many of us believe His accusations.

Often, we are so blindsided by his attacks that all we can do is huddle in the corner he has backed us in and quake in fear as he continues to roar in our face. Many times, during the onslaught of the attack, we barely strength to attempt to fight off the fog and vice like grip of the oppression and depression that follows on the heels of Satan's rampage.

It's difficult to remember that you are not who and what he's accused you of being, it's difficult not to believe what he tells you. The truth is we are - as a human being - messed up depraved, evil. However, due to the believer's faith in Christ and His finished work, we are cleansed, washed, holy, sanctified, being sanctified, justified and one day we will be glorified! While we fail and fall into sin at times, we are not the sum of our faults and failures. We are a son or daughter of God. We are a royal priesthood, we are a peculiar people, we are God's workmanship, we are the apple of His eye! We must hold fast to our faith and believe what God says about us - not what Satan says about us! When the doubts of sin assail, Heaven's grace will never fail! When Satan attacks, use the name of Jesus to defend yourself! There's power in His name!

Don't think on past failures - whether fifty years ago or five seconds ago. If you have repented, they are gone, wiped away, erased by the blood of Jesus

Christ! God will never bring them up to you again. Instead, think on things that are pure, lovely and of a good report. In other words, think on Christ! Think of all He has done, all He brought you through. Think on these things!

~*~ Finally Brethren, whatsoever things are true, whatsoever things are honest, whatsoever things are just, whatsoever things are pure, whatsoever things are lovely, whatsoever things are of good report; if there be any virtue, if there be any praise, think on these things.
Philippians 4:8 ~*~

~*~ For God has not given us the spirit of fear; but of power, and of love, and of a sound mind.
2 Timothy 1:7 ~*~

~*~ For as many as are led by the Spirit of God, they are the sons of God. For you have not received the spirit of bondage again to fear; but you have received the Spirit of Adoption, whereby we cry, Abba, Father.
Romans 8:14-15 ~*~

RIGHT FAITH, WRONG FOCUS

We live in a world of constant busyness. Run here, do this, call there, fix that - the list seems unending. Everyday, we are bombarded by things that, while important, often receive a wrongful place and priority in our life. Thus, we tend to lose focus of what really matters - the Lord and our relationship with Him.

Even when our faith is right, our focus can still be wrong. Our faith is in the Lord for all things, but our focus may be a job, our business, a better house, a better car, seeking a spouse, etc. There is nothing wrong with wanting to succeed on your job or in business - but that shouldn't be your focus. It's perfectly fine to want a bigger house and better car - but that shouldn't be your focus. There's nothing wrong with wanting to be married - but marriage should not be your focus. Christ is to be our focus.

David said, I have set the Lord always before me. There were times when David veered way off course. Once, his focus was a married woman and he was so set on having her for himself that he not only had an affair with her, but he also arranged for her husband to be killed. Wrong focus will throw us off course and it often leads to sin. Yet, it seems David learned a great deal, because he declares that he has set the Lord always before him. What happened? David was convicted and readjusted his focus.

When someone is set before you, they are in front of you, meaning your eyes are constantly on them, your steps mirror their steps. It's time we sharpen our focus. Our faith is in Christ and His finished work; it's time our focus lined up with our faith.

~*~ I have set the Lord always before me: because He is at my right hand, I shall not be moved.

Psalm 16:8 ~*~

Our Refuge

During our Christian walk, there will be times when we face storms. Often, they catch us unawares. One moment, the sea of life is calm and sailing smooth and the next, the waves of testing and trial threaten to overtake us.

These trials, these storms can come in any form - physical, mental, emotional, domestic, financial. Regardless of which form they take - one thing is for certain: we will need a shelter, a refuge from the storm.

When these storms come our way, we need not only a refuge from the storm, but we also need an anchor in the midst of the storm. We need something that - no matter how rough the sea, no matter the howling winds and boisterous waves - won't break. We need an anchor that will keep our vessel afloat and holds us steadfast and sure.

We can count on two things in this life: Satan will send storms to shipwreck our faith, but our Anchor - Jesus Christ - won't let our ship sink! We are anchored in Him and through Him, we are able to weather any storm.

~*~ God is our refuge and strength, a very present help in trouble. Therefore will not we fear, though the Earth be removed and though the mountains be carried into the midst of the sea; though the waters thereof roar and be troubled, though the mountains shake with the swelling thereof. Selah.
Psalm 46:1-3 ~*~

Encouraged in the Lord

If you are on the battlefield for the Lord, you're a target for Satan. If you're saved, but have not been anything other than a pew warmer, Satan isn't as concerned with you because you pose little threat to him. However, for those fighting on the front lines in this battle, Satan will attack ferociously. His main target is your faith.

However the attacks may manifest - physical, emotional, financial - the root of the attack is spiritual. He will hit you with discouragement to the point you almost give up, because if he can get you to quit believing, if he can steal your faith, then he has you right where he wants you.

You may be a pastor, an evangelist or you may be a housewife who witnesses to her unsaved neighbors. Whoever you are, wherever you are - if you are about the Father's business, Satan will attack you with discouragement.

Yet, when we are discouraged, the craziness of this world gets overwhelming and the spears of the enemy surround us on every side, we have hope - His name is Jesus, Wonderful Counselor, Mighty God, the Prince of Peace.

We can encourage ourselves in the fact that despite our circumstances, no matter what we face, God is faithful. In an ever changing world, He is the unchangeable One.

~*~ And David was greatly distressed, for the people spake of stoning him, because the soul of all the people was grieved, every man for his sons and for his daughters: but David encouraged himself in the Lord his God
1 Samuel 30:6 ~*~

Lord, I Believe

I've lost count of the times in my own life that I've prayed a prayer very much like the father in Mark chapter nine. "I didn't see the storm coming, but Lord I believe!" "I didn't expect this to happen, but Lord I believe!" "Lord, I don't understand this, but I trust You!" The unspoken cry of my heart was always, "Lord, help me to keep believing!"

When you're tossed on an unending sea of trouble, will you still believe? Even when it seems like you're surrounded by the enemy on every side, will you still choose to trust? Though you may quake in fear, raise a heartfelt cry to your Heavenly Father and say, "Lord, I believe! Help me to keep believing!" You will feel faith begin to rise up and fear will begin to disappear! Lord, I believe!!

~*~ Jesus said unto him, If thou canst believe, all things are possible to him that believeth. And straightway the father of the child cried out, and said with tears, Lord, I believe; help Thou mine unbelief.

Mark 9:23-24 ~*~

Forgiveness

Throughout my life, I have had to forgive people for wrongs, betrayals, for being mean and hateful and a host of other things. During this same time, I have also needed the forgiveness of the Lord and others.

Forgiveness isn't easy. Betrayal, lies, half truths, words that wound, mean spiritedness - all of these things and many more are difficult to forgive because they are an offense to us. The offended party, the victim, the innocent person feels they shouldn't have to forgive - either because the betrayal was too great or because they don't think the other person deserves forgiveness. I readily admit that some things are really difficult to forgive. However, I have learned some things about forgiveness.

Forgive even if they don't apologize. It doesn't matter if they never apologize, that has no bearing on the forgiveness offered them.

Forgiveness doesn't excuse their wrong action, their sin against you. It is not saying that what they did was acceptable. What it does say is holding on to the hurt and anger isn't worth it.

You will need forgiveness too. At some point, you are going to fail the Lord and you're going to need His forgiveness. However, not forgiven those who have offended you, then God cannot and will not forgive you. Holding on to an offense is not worth you losing your soul.

~*~ For if you forgive men their trespasses, your heavenly Father will also forgive you: But if you forgive not men their trespasses, neither will your Father forgive your trespasses.

Matthew 6:14-15 ~*~

ALL CONSUMING FIRE

It seems the church has lost its reverence for God. Where once we used to stand in awe of all He is, all He has done and all He is able to do; we not point angry fingers at God and shake an angry fist at Him when we don't get our way.

We have lost all sense of Godly fear. Once, there were true worshipers, now we go to church and "play the part" and "perform" our "due service" for the Lord by showing up to church. Listen, if the only reason you're going to church is out of some weird sense of duty, you may as well stay home.

We used to want to be consumed by God and were consumed by the things of God. Now, we are consumed with worldly lusts. Let us turn again to our first Love. Let us fall at His feet in humble repentance, crying out to Him. Then let us completely lose ourselves in His presence and once again be consumed by the all consuming fire that is our God.

~*~ Wherefore we receiving a kingdom which cannot be moved, let us have grace whereby we may serve God acceptably with reverence and godly fear: for our God is a consuming fire
                              Hebrews 12:28-29 ~*~

A Love Worth Receiving

Jesus thinks we are worth loving, His blood says we are worth it. Despite our willfulness, despirt us going our own way - despite US - He still loves us, still heals us, still intercedes for us, still sees our tears and wraps us in arms of love. O, what a Savior!

~*~ The Lord hath appeared of old unto me, saying, Yeah, I have loved thee with an everlasting love: therefore with lovingkindness have I drawn thee.
Jeremiah 31:3 ~*~

Godly Wisdom

Just because someone holds hate in their heart doesn't mean you should. Don't let their bitterness turn you sour. At the end of the day, their hatefulness and bitterness is what keeps them company. A person with a heart full of love and compassion who has not allowed the trials of life to corrupt their sweet spirit will lay down and sleep in sweet peace. People will be mean, cruel even - but we don't have to allow their hate to infect our hearts. Choose to dance in the rain, praise through the pain and sing through the sorrow.

~*~ But the wisdom that is from above is first pure, then peaceable, gentle, and easy to be intreated, full of mercy and good fruits, without partiality, and without hypocrisy.

James 3:17 ~*~

BEAUTY FOR ASHES

Jesus makes beauty from ashes. He makes broken things, broken people whole. He takes dead hearts, dead lives, dead hopes, dead dreams and with just the touch of His hand - revives them. To the hopeless, He is that bright ray of hope. To the fatherless, He is a Father. To the forgotten, afraid and alone, He is the Comforter. To the beaten, battered and bruised, He is the soothing Balm of Gilead. No matter what you've gone through, no matter the abuse, scars and bruises, Jesus loves you and He died to make you whole in every way. He is the Great Physician, but He can only heal those who will come to Him for healing.

Often we think Jesus couldn't possibly want anything to do with us. We're a mess and we know we are at times such a failure at trying to live for Him. The Lord isn't looking for perfection in us; He's looking for a heart that is faithful to Him. He's looking for a heart that burns for Him and His kingdom. Come to Him and let Him turn your wretchedness into blessedness, your mourning into dancing, your sorrow into joy and your ashes into beauty. For all those broken promises, Jesus is the Promise Keeper. For all those mountains that need to be moved, He is the Way Maker. He's the Miracle Worker and the Light in the midst of your darkest trial. When you feel you can't make it, He is strong in your brokenness.

~*~ The Spirit of the Lord God is upon me; because the Lord hath anointed me to preach good tidings unto the meek; he hath sent me to bind up the brokenhearted, to proclaim liberty to the captives, and the opening of the prison to them that are bound; To proclaim the acceptable year of the Lord, and the day of vengeance of our God; to comfort all that mourn; To appoint unto them that mourn in Zion, to give unto them beauty for ashes, the oil of joy for mourning, the garment of praise for the spirit of heaviness; that they might be called trees of righteousness, the planting of the Lord, that he might be glorified.

Isaiah 61:1-3 ~*~

Balm of Gilead

The human heart searches and ponders many things: the meaning of life, our purpose, who we will marry, how we fit into this great universe. The ponderings are endless. Yet, for all our pondering, we find no answers to the questions of life. Finally, we come full circle and ponder almost the exact thing we've pondered countless times before. It's one question; just four little words, yet the enormity of the question is quite staggering. Why am I here?

It's one thing to ask the question, but to set out trying to answer that question through every earthly pleasure? That's something altogether different. The ponderings of the human heart cannot be answered by vain philosophy or psychology. In fact, no human being can answer the questions in the heart of another human. No earthly pleasure can satisfy or fill the void in the human heart and soul. There is but one Answer, one Solution - His name is Jesus Christ. For every question, He is the Answer. Christ is the missing piece of the puzzle that is life. There is no place for confusion when you have the Author of Divine Order living within you.

For every cut, bruise and wound, He is the healing Balm of Gilead. The writer asked the question, "Is there no balm in Gilead? Is there no physician there?" I say unto you, yes - there most certainly is a healing Balm in Gilead, for I have experienced His wonder working power in my life, His healing more times than I can number.

There is a Balm in Gilead. There is an Answer for all your ponderings. There is One called Jesus Christ. He is alive and well and He's walking on the troubled waters of your life. The storm may rage, but He speaks peace be still to you.

~*~ Is there no balm in Gilead; is there no physician there?
Jeremiah 8:22a ~*~

A Good Soldier

Our journey through a land troubled with hurt, sorrow, pain, misunderstanding, hatred, woe and bitterness can get lonely. We are saved, the Lord is always with us - but sometimes, we are void of human companionship. We often find we have no real friends - only fair weather friends. We often struggle to understand why friends and even family forsake us. Yet, even in the midst of this we must march on.

We don't march in our own strength, but in the strength of Christ. We don't march to the beat of our own drum, but to the heartbeat of the One who died for us. We march on, determined to cross the finish line and one day hear Him say, "Well done". Can we be found faithful when all others forsake us? Can we be found faithful when we don't understand God's plan? Will we be found faithful when we don't see or feel God working?

The mark of a soldier of the cross is never more apparent than when they face obstacle after obstacle, trial after trial, test after test, heartbreak after heartbreak and they still keep their faith in Christ.

When you're tested, tried and broken, will you still trust His heart even when you don't see His plan? Will you still stand, assured that He loves you, even as the storm rages around you? When we trust the Lord - when we trust His love, His will, His plans for us - then even in the midst of extreme adversity, we can stand and truly say, "Though He slay me, yet will I trust in Him."

~*~ Thou therefore endure hardness, as a good soldier of Jesus Christ.
2 Timothy 2:3 ~*~

Unlimited Mercy

The faithfulness of God is proven time and time again; His promises hold fast no matter the turmoil or storm. His mercy is new every morning. This means that every morning when you open your eyes and before you ever get out of bed, there's a fresh supply of God's mercy waiting for you. You don't have to beg Him for it. If you belong to Him, His mercy is there for you.

His mercy isn't proven by the absence of trouble, but rather that He has brought us through time and time again. The fact that He never fails to provide new mercy each day is a testimony of God's faithfulness to His children. His mercy is a spiritual renewable resource that we access every day by faith.

There will never be a day when we wake up and God says, "Sorry, I completely forgot to renew mercy for you today" or "You woke up late and you missed out on mercy for today". God is faithful and because He is the faithful God - as His children, we have a never ending supply of His mercy 0 because we've been washed in Calvary's precious fountain.

~*~ This I recall to my mind, therefore have I hope. It is of the Lord's mercies that we are not consumed, because His compassions fail not. They are new every morning: great is Thy faithfulness.
                                    Lamentations 3:21-23~*~

To Know Him

We do not possess the wisdom or understanding to truly know God. He wants us to know Him - so He makes Himself known by revealing Himself to us in many ways. He reveals Himself through His Word, through His Presence - but most of all - He reveals Himself through His Son.

If you want to know God, get in His Word, get in His Presence - but most importantly - be found in Christ. Your faith in Christ, your relationship with Him will draw you closer to God and you will know God in a greater way than you have ever imagined.

~*~ For God, who commanded the light to shine out of darkness, hath shined in our hearts, to give the light of the knowledge of the glory of God in the face of Jesus Christ.
2 Corinthians 4:6 ~*~

~*~ And hope maketh not ashamed; because the love of God is shed abroad in our hearts by the Holy Ghost which is given unto us.
Romans 5:5 ~*~

GRACE UPON GRACE

There is a love that transcends time and eternity. There is a love that is gentle, yet fierce in its strength. There is a love that is unconditional and fathomless in its endurance and beauty. There is a love that offers a warm embrace, yet also demands chastisement. There is a love that is a refuge and strong tower. There is a love that is a lighthouse in the midst of the storm, a haven of rest from the trials of life.

There is a love that rescues and pardons. There is a love that welcomes the prodigal. There is a love that spreads wide its arms to the forgotten. There is a love that offers forgiveness, yet demands repentance. There is a love that binds up the wounds of the soul. There is a love that heals the brokenness of the spirit.

There is a love that demands justice, yet met those demands on the cross where Jesus died in our place. There is a love that offers unlimited mercy and grace upon grace.

~*~ And the Word was made flesh, and dwelt among us, (and we beheld His glory, the glory as of the only begotten of the Father,) full of grace and truth. John bare witness of Him, and cried, saying, This was He of whom I spake, He that cometh after me is preferred before me: for He was before me. And of His fulness have all we received, and grace for grace. For the law was given by Moses, but grace and truth came by Jesus Christ.

John 1:14-17 ~*~

HE SATISFIES THE LONGING SOUL

There is a void in the heart and soul of every human being. We so foolishly try to fill that void with the things of this world. We are seeking fulfillment in every place, from everyone and everything except the only One who can truly fill that void. We find ourselves bound by heartache and pain because we have tied ourselves to the world, seeking from it what only Jesus Christ can add to us. His goodness toward us, His wonderful works that are beyond our comprehension - all of these are the fingerprints of the Lord in our lives.

If your soul is longing for true goodness and fulfillment, you won't find it in the world or anything the world offers. If your soul is hungry, the world cannot offer you proper nourishment. All the world offers is temporary pleasures, but in the right hand of the Lord of Glory are pleasures forevermore. In Christ alone is found all that we need for life and living. He is the fulfillment of our every longing. He is the Manna that satisfies our hungry soul. There's not one person who has ever come to the Master's table in faith and walked away unfulfilled. Truly, He does satisfy.

~*~ Oh that men would praise the Lord for His goodness, and for His wonderful works to the children of men! For He satisfieth the longing soul, and filleth the hungry soul with goodness.

Psalm 107:8-9 ~*~

His Purpose

We all long to see God's good purpose in our lives. It's so much easier to see God's good purpose in the easy things, in the things that are good. The difficult part is seeing God's good purpose in the hard times. Where's the good purpose in our brokenness? Where's the good purpose in our pain? Where's the good purpose in our trials? That's not so easy to see.

Even though we cannot see God's good purpose in the hurting, we have to trust that He does have a good purpose. He never promised things would always be good. He never promised life would be easy. He did promise that if we love Him, He would work all things together for our good. He did promise that He is with us, even in the most trying of times. He did promise He'd never leave us nor forsake us.

What if the pain you're suffering today will be the testimony you share that helps someone through the valley tomorrow? What if the brokenness you feel right now is really the beginning of God's preparation for the calling He has on your life? There is no testimony without a test, there is no true praise without pain and there is no calling without a cost. Lift up your head, child of God, for He has a good purpose in all things that He allows to happen in your life. Keep trusting Him, and soon, you will see His good purpose.

~*~ And we know that all things work together for good to them that love God, to them who are the called according to His purpose.
Romans 8:28 ~*~

Unlimited Supply

Whatever you're searching for, whatever you need - you will find it in God's riches in glory. It doesn't matter much you need or how often you need a refill, God's got it. Whatever the need, the blood of Jesus Christ has already made the provision for you.

If you need more grace, God's got it. If you need more mercy, His mercy is new every morning. If you need strength, He offers His joy to strengthen you. If you need healing, the blood of Jesus Christ paid for it. If you need a financial miracle, God has the provision you need. The benefits of Christ's finished work can never be exhausted; God's supply never runs out. Whatever the need, there is an unlimited supply for you - but it's only found in God's riches by and through Christ Jesus.

~*~ But my God shall supply all your need according to His riches in glory by Christ Jesus.

Philippians 4:19 ~*~

THE COUNSEL OF THE LORD

Why do we seek answers from everyone other than the One who truly has the answer? Why do we seek solutions to life's problems from every resource except the true Source of wisdom?

The advice of our fellow man, while meant to help - can offer little help or hope unless they are giving advice straight from God's word. The wisdom of man can never solve man's problems. However, the wisdom of God not only brings the answer we've been searching for and the solutions we've been seeking, but it also brings peace and understanding. That's why Jesus is called the Wonderful Counselor. His advice is always good. His wisdom is always best and His counsel will always stand.

~*~ There are many devices in a man's heart; nevertheless the counsel of the Lord, that shall stand.

Proverbs 19:21 ~*~

BLESSINGS IN CHRIST

We are often guilty of seeking physical blessings above spiritual blessings. God wants us to prosper in every way, but the key is that prosperity will only come as our soul prospers. Souls are what matter the most to God, and He longs to give those spiritual blessings to help us in our daily walk. He offers them freely, but we have to want them, we have to willingly receive them. He will never force anything on us that we don't want - including His spiritual blessings.

When our soul is prospering, when we are basking in the spiritual blessings of God, we will begin to see prosperity in other areas of our lives as well. This is true prosperity. Your soul prospers as you walk with the Lord, accepting all the wonderful spiritual blessings that Jesus died to provide. He doesn't just long to give us a few spiritual blessings - He longs to give us all spiritual blessings that are found only in Christ.

~*~ Blessed be the God and Father of our Lord Jesus Christ, who hath blessed us with all spiritual blessings in heavenly places in Christ
Ephesians 1:3 ~*~

The Path of Life

We are all on a journey, but the choices we make determine our destination. At some point during our lives, we are going to be given the chance to choose the path of eternal life or the path of eternal damnation. This is the most important decision we will ever make and it has the potential of having eternal rewards or eternal consequences.

If we choose to follow Christ, He will show us the path of life. He doesn't just show us the path, though. He also goes down that path ahead of us, leading us all the way. While we are on this path of life with our Savior, we find complete joy in His presence, every need is supplied and we find pleasures that last for eternity.

~*~ Thou wilt shew me the path of life: in Thy presence is fulness of joy; at Thy right hand there are pleasures for evermore.
Psalm 16:11 ~*~

The Blessing of the Lord

The Lord blesses those who follow Him. He blesses those who are obedient to Him and are faithful to heed His voice. These blessings from the Lord are the best, sent from the riches of Heaven. They come in a wide variety, but they all come to the believer because of their faith in Jesus Christ - the One who died to provide those blessings.

While life has its ups and downs and the Christian is not exempt, the blessings the Lord sends along the way bring joy and not sorrow. They will not be a weight on our back, nor will they be a noose around our neck. The blessings of the Lord enrich our lives - spiritually, physically, mentally, emotionally, domestically - and there's no strings attached. He freely gives to us because we belong to Him.

~*~ The blessing of the Lord, it maketh rich, and he addeth no sorrow with it.

Proverbs 10:22 ~*~

THE GOD OF HOPE

Faith is a wonderful thing, when it's properly placed. To be saved, we must exhibit faith in Christ and what He did for us on Calvary's cross. When we do this, not only do we receive salvation, but we are now able to receive all the benefits that Jesus died to give us. We now have been reconciled to the God of hope. He is the Originator of our hope and He is faithful to fill us with all joy and peace as long as we keep believing.

Faith in Christ brings salvation, but along with salvation comes all these wonderful things that we would have never had access to had we not accepted Christ as Lord and Savior. We are promised that we will abound in hope. This hope doesn't come by means of our own strength, but it comes the same way our salvation came - by faith. When we have our faith in Christ, we abound in hope through the power of the Holy Ghost! The God of hope, promises us so many wonderful things if we will only believe and then He empowers us by the Holy Ghost to abound in that hope that He promised. That's the God we serve!

~*~ Now the God of hope fill you with all joy and peace in believing, that ye may abound in hope, through the power of the Holy Ghost.
Romans 15:13 ~*~

CAST YOUR BURDENS ON THE LORD

Life isn't without its burdens. Sometimes just the weight of living in a world that refuses to honor God, but rather desires to exalt self is enough to make us long for our Heavenly home. It makes us long to be by our Savior's side in glory, where we never have to be troubled with burdens again.

While we are here on Earth, we are to cast our burdens upon the Lord. In other words, we do more than just lay them down or put them away to fret over another day. We actually throw those burdens to Jesus. Financial burden? Throw that burden to Jesus! Family problems? Throw those burdens to Jesus! Weak and weary from the trials of life? Throw those burdens to Jesus! Hurt and wounded by those you love? Throw those burdens to Jesus!

The promise was never a life void of trouble. The promise was never a life void of burdens and cares. The promise has always been that the Lord will sustain those who throw their burdens on Him. The promise has always been that the righteous will not be moved. Roots run deep, and when you are firmly planted in Christ, you will stand. No matter what you face in this life, you will remain steadfast because you are anchored in the One who will never allow you to be moved.

~*~ Cast thy burden upon the Lord, and he shall sustain thee: he shall never suffer the righteous to be moved.

Psalms 55:22 ~*~

In Everything Give Thanks

God has a plan for each life. His will for each individual person is different according to His plans for them. However, there are some things that are the same for every believer.

God's will is that every believer rejoice evermore, pray without ceasing and give thanks in everything. In these three things, we find God giving the answer to life's problems. No matter what we go through, we are to continue to rejoice in the Lord. This doesn't mean that we are rejoicing where the problem is concerned, but we are rejoicing continually in the One we know is able to bring us through. We are to pray without ceasing. Pray about everything, all the time. Seek the Lord's wisdom in your decision making, seek Him in every situation. We are to give thanks in everything. We often confuse this with giving thanks for everything. That's not what we are told to do - we are told to give thanks in everything. That means no matter what valley we go through, no matter the mountains we have to climb, we are to be in a constant state of thanksgiving to God.

Rejoice, pray, give thanks, repeat. This should be consistent in the life of every believer. When we do these three things, we will find that our spirits are no longer heavy, but lightened because we are constantly finding ourselves in the presence of God, which gives no place to the devil.

~*~ Rejoice evermore. Pray without ceasing. In every thing give thanks: for this is the will of God in Christ Jesus concerning you.
1 Thessalonians 5:16-18 ~*~

Seek the Lord

To truly understand all things, we need a wisdom that is lightyears beyond ours. We need infinite wisdom that searches and knows the motives of every heart at any given time. We need the wisdom of the Lord.

We cannot understand anything pertaining to spiritual matters if we don't know the Lord. We must have His help to open our blinded eyes, we need Him to remove the blinders that have made us indifferent to sin, so we will be able to see it plainly.

If we are still carnally minded - unsaved - we cannot understand judgment or anything that pertains to the things of God. If we will choose Christ, if we will seek the Lord, He will bring us an understanding of all things. He will impart His wisdom to all who place their faith in Him.

~*~ Evil men understand not judgment: but they that seek the Lord understand all things.

Proverbs 28:5 ~*~

He Goes Before You

There are many questions for tomorrow. There are many questions about the future. We must trust those all to the Lord. He has promised that He will go before us and will make the crooked places straight. He has promised to free us from our bondage and to give us treasures and hidden riches of secret places. He has promised to do this to prove to us that He is the One who calls us by name and He is the God of Israel.

Don't worry about tomorrow, live in today. Before you ever reach tomorrow, the Lord goes before you. He's already in your tomorrow, fighting for you before you ever arrive. He is faithful and so very protective over His children. So He goes before us, preparing the way before we ever get to tomorrow. There's nothing that you faced today that caught the Lord by surprise. There's nothing you will face tomorrow that He has not already made a way for.

~*~ I will go before thee, and make the crooked places straight: I will break in pieces the gates of brass, and cut in sunder the bars of iron: And I will give thee the treasures of darkness, and hidden riches of secret places, that thou mayest know that I, the Lord, which call thee by thy name, am the God of Israel.

Isaiah 45:2-3 ~*~

GOD OF ALL POWER

He who formed the mountains is the same One who formed you from the dust of the ground. The same One who created the wind is the One who breathed breath into your nostrils. The same God who knows your every thought, has wonderful plans for your life. The same God who treads on the high places of the Earth is the same One who tenderly watches over you. The same hands that pushed up mountains and scooped out seas are the very same hands that hold us when we are broken.

How amazing that the God of all power, of such magnificent strength and might is so tender and gentle with His children. The same God who demands justice is also the very One who reaches way down to pick us up. The same One who parted the Red Sea and pushed down the Jericho walls is also the One who draws us to His side and tenderly ministers to all our wounded and bruised places. Hands so strong and capable, hands of such great power also show such grace, mercy and restraint when dealing with His most prized possession - His children. What a mighty God we serve!

~*~ For, lo, He that formeth the mountains, and createth the wind, and declareth unto man what is his thought, that maketh the morning darkness, and treadeth upon the high places of the earth, The Lord, The God of hosts, is His name.

Amos 4:13 ~*~

ABOUT THE AUTHOR

Humbled and honored that the Lord would use her to reach others, Becky stands in awe of what He has done in her life - and she knows He's not finished yet. Called and anointed of the Lord to preach and teach, Becky sought Him for direction concerning ministry. The Lord answered those heartfelt prayers for guidance and Restoration Ministries was born. Soon after, Becky began teaching an online Bible study class after church on Sunday. After two years, Becky felt the Lord was leading Restoration Ministries in a different direction. For over a year now, Becky has been sharing live teachings via social media, sharing the good news of the Gospel with anyone who will listen. When asked what makes her special, Becky says, "There's nothing special about me. I'm human just like you; I fail, I make mistakes. I'm just an imperfect country girl who is in love with a perfect, holy God. Just because I'm called to preach the Gospel of Jesus Christ doesn't mean I'm automatically perfect. No - far from it! I'm not a completed work, I'm a work in progress. I love God, I love His Word and I love people. I am a yielded vessel in the hands of the Lord". When speaking of the heart of Restoration Ministries, Becky states, "Restoration Ministries' mission is found in Mark 16:15 '....Go ye into all the world, and preach the Gospel to every creature.' It's about souls, it's about spreading the Gospel - the liberating Message of the Cross far and wide, it's about going out into the highways and hedges and compelling them to come in. Time is so, so short and the harvest is ripe! I am preaching the Message of the Cross until every ear has heard, every heart has been stirred and every chain is broken." When she's not encouraging brothers and sisters in the Lord or reaching the lost with the Gospel, Becky enjoys being around all kinds of animals - especially horses and dogs; she also enjoys hiking, nature, reading, singing and cooking. Becky says, "I just enjoy life because God is good!"

Made in the USA
Middletown, DE
25 May 2021

40359548R00038